GASES

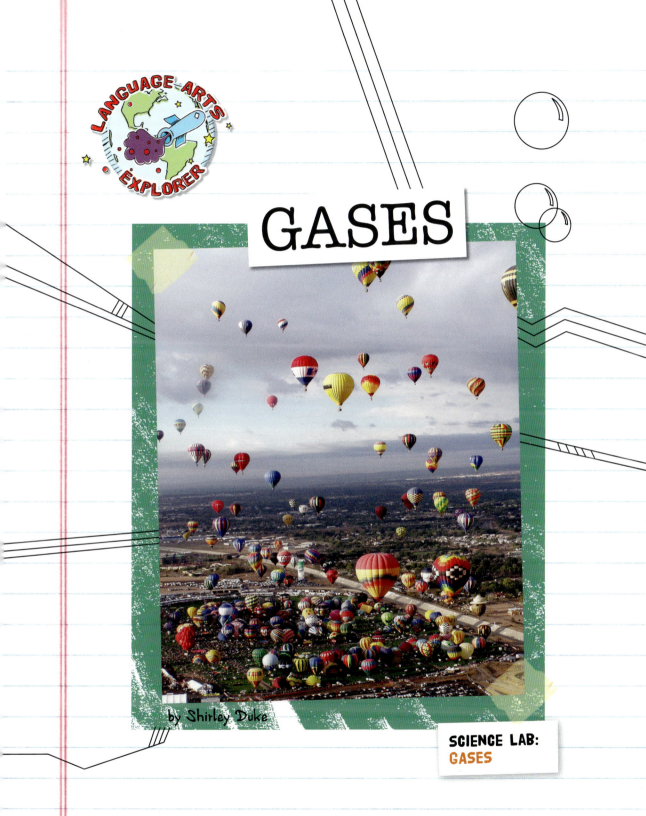

by Shirley Duke

SCIENCE LAB:
GASES

CHERRY LAKE PUBLISHING • ANN ARBOR, MICHIGAN

Published in the United States of America
by Cherry Lake Publishing
Ann Arbor, Michigan
www.cherrylakepublishing.com

Printed in the United States of America
Corporate Graphics Inc
September 2011
CLFA09

Consultants: Griffith Jones, clinical associate professor, College of Education, University of Florida; Gail Saunders-Smith, associate professor of literacy, Beeghly College of Education, Youngstown University

Editorial direction: Book design and illustration:
Lisa Owings   Kazuko Collins

Photo credits: David James/Shutterstock Images, cover; Pawel Libera/Photolibrary, 5; Jose AS Reyes/Shutterstock Images, 6; Shutterstock Images, 7; Bob Child/AP Images, 9; Marek Mnich/iStockphoto, 12; Gary Kazanjian/AP Images, 14; Red Line Editorial, 16; Cliff Parnell/iStockphoto, 19; Bonnie Avonrude/Dreamstime, 21; Yang Yu/Fotolia, 24; Ilja Mašík/Shutterstock Images, 27

Library of Congress Cataloging-in-Publication Data
Duke, Shirley Smith.
  Science lab. Gases / by Shirley Duke.
      p. cm. – (Language arts explorer. Science lab)
  Includes index.
  ISBN 978-1-61080-203-1 – ISBN 978-1-61080-292-5 (pbk.)
  1. Gases–Juvenile literature. I. Title. II. Title: Gases.
  TP242.D85 2011
  533–dc23
                                    2011015128

Cherry Lake Publishing would like to acknowledge the work of The Partnership for 21st Century Skills. Please visit www.21stCenturySkills.org for more information.

TABLE OF CONTENTS

You are being given a mission. The facts in What You Know will help you accomplish it. Remember the clues from What You Know while you are reading the story. The clues and the story will help you answer the questions at the end of the book. Have fun on this adventure!

Your mission is to explore what gases are and how they act. What can gases do? How do scientists learn about gases? What kinds of experiments help us understand how gases behave? What effects do gases have on the environment? Review the facts in What You Know, and then start your mission to discover why gases are so important.

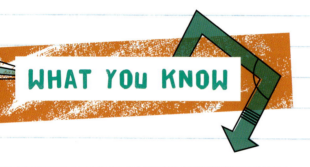

WHAT YOU KNOW

★ Gas **molecules** move in straight lines until they collide with other molecules and spread out. Gas molecules spread much farther apart than liquid molecules.

★ Gases have no shape or size. They spread out to fill their container.

★ Gases exert pressure on their surroundings.

★ The motion and energy of gases increase when they are heated, making them expand, and decrease when they are cooled, making them contract.

You can learn more about gases outside the classroom. Gases are all around you!

★ Gases are easy to **compress** because they are so spread out. The more a gas is compressed, the stronger its pressure becomes.

Maria Lee is researching gases for an article in *Chemistry Kids* magazine. She's meeting with experts to learn about gases and what they do. Carry out your mission by reading her journal.

I've never studied gases, so I begin my research at Wilson High School in Flagstaff, Arizona. I'm meeting with chemistry teacher Amy Jones in her science lab. Mrs. Jones starts our interview with a series of demonstrations. She asks me to stand at the front of the room, and she takes a covered test tube filled with liquid to the back of the room. She opens the test tube, holds it up, and asks me if I smell anything.

Gas molecules spread out to fill their container. The container could be as small as a balloon or as big as Earth's atmosphere.

"No, I don't," I reply. She waits. After about thirty seconds, I tell her I smell ammonia. Before I can ask her what this means, she walks over to me and hands me a balloon. She tells me to blow it up and tie a knot at the opening. I set the filled balloon on the table.

"Now watch," Mrs. Jones says. She takes my balloon and places it in a cooler filled with dry ice. After a minute, she pulls the balloon from the cooler. It has shrunk to half its original size. "What happened?" I ask.

"Just a minute. We have something else to do," she tells me. She takes a peeled boiled egg and covers it with

Dry ice is the solid form of carbon dioxide gas. When dry ice melts, it becomes a gas instead of a liquid.

oil. Next she lights a match and drops it into the narrow opening of a glass bottle. She sets the egg on top of the opening. All of a sudden, I hear a little puff. The egg wobbles a bit and then slips down into the jar—whole! I can't believe it. But before I can ask why, she offers me a can of soda.

"I'd love one," I say. She takes my soda, shakes it, and then hands it to me. She smiles. "You'd better tap the top before you open it." I tap the top and open the drink. It fizzes a little but doesn't spill over. I wonder what all these demonstrations mean.

Mrs. Jones says I've seen what gases can do and invites me back after I've finished the rest of my interviews. If I still don't understand her demonstrations, she promises to explain them when I return. She says scientists learn by observing, experimenting, and asking questions. I leave, eager to find out more about gases. ★

Still puzzling over the demonstrations, I travel to the San Joaquin Valley in California. I meet atmospheric chemist Tony Hernandez in a huge field of beans.

"My job is to find out if the air here is dirty or clean," says Tony. "I use special equipment to sample the air in the

Atmospheric chemists use special equipment to take samples of the air. They can run tests to determine pollutants.

valley." He shows me a suitcase-sized box. "An opening in the box lets air enter. We can identify the gases present in the air by the way the gases interact with chemicals inside the box. Back at the lab, I'll run tests to find out which gases are polluting the air."

He says that there are many kinds of gases. Air is made of several different gases. It is 78 percent nitrogen, 21 percent oxygen, and around one percent other gases. That one percent includes **water vapor**, or water in its gas form.

"What is a gas, exactly?" I ask. Tony replies that gases are one state of matter. Solids and liquids are also states of matter. Unlike solids, gases don't have a shape of their own. Gas molecules spread out because they are constantly moving and bumping into other molecules. If there's no container to stop them, the molecules continue spreading out in the atmosphere. Liquids also take the shape of their container, but their molecules are bound closer together than in gases. Gas molecules move freely through the air.

"What gases are you checking for?" I ask.

He grins. "Just the bad ones. Nitrogen oxides and sulfur dioxides are gases that pollute the air," Tony says. "When they mix with oxygen, they can become acidic. Acidic gases are harmful to the environment."

"How can they hurt the environment by just floating around in the air?" I ask.

"Acidic gases cling to water molecules. They float through the air until they find a raindrop to ride on. The acidic drops of water land on plants like these beans. The acid damages leaves, which harms the plant's ability to make food and grow. But acid rain affects much more than just plants," Tony says. "It hurts animals and people too. Acid rain is especially harmful when it falls in ponds or lakes." I ask Tony where acidic gases come from. Have they always been part of our atmosphere, or did someone create them?

ACID RAIN DISASTER

In the 1970s, large amounts of acid rain fell over the northeastern United States. This rain killed trees and fish, dissolved layers of stone buildings, and caused lung damage in humans. Laws were passed to control the amounts of harmful gases going into the air. After 20 years, acidic gas pollution was cut in half. More reductions occurred in 2000, and most places have recovered from acid rain damage.

Tony tells me acid rain was first noticed in the 1800s. Coal-burning factories put the acidic gases in the air. The gases drifted with the wind and attached to water molecules, raining down on plants, lakes, and ponds far away from the factories. I understand. Gas molecules keep bumping into one another and spreading out until their particles are in the air across the country. I think about Mrs. Jones's ammonia. I smelled it because gases spread through the air.

Acid rain can kill an entire forest.

"Do you check for pollutants every day?" I ask. Tony replies that he checks once a week. He records the levels and kinds of pollutants on his laptop computer. Keeping track of this information over long periods of time helps him monitor changes. He reports any changes to the Environmental Protection Agency.

I say good-bye to Tony and leave the bean field. I have more questions about gases and their properties than when I started. Now I understand that gases move outward in all directions. But harmful gases spread this way too. I will have to wait until my next stop to find out more. ★

Today I'm at a dairy farm outside Modesto, California. My nose lets me know before I get to the main barn! The farm odors remind me of the smell coming from the open test tube at Wilson High School. The ammonia particles spread out, just like the farm odors. Acidic gases move through the air in the same way.

Dave Kent greets me and invites me into the barn. Cows line the stalls, chewing away at their food. I see grates

Some large dairy farms have found a way to turn animal waste into usable energy.

behind them. Dave says manure and other wastes drain through the grates and are flushed into holding pits called lagoons. We walk past the cows, and he opens a door at the back of the barn. I smell the lagoons before I see them. Dave laughs when he sees my wrinkled nose.

"They might smell bad, but they are part of the solution to a big problem. Cows produce large amounts of **methane**. Methane is a gas, so it spreads throughout the earth's atmosphere," he says.

"What's wrong with that?" I ask.

"The problem is that methane is a **greenhouse gas**. That means it traps the sun's heat. Too much methane in the atmosphere can cause the earth to get too warm. Earth's climate has already begun to change. Small changes

THE GREENHOUSE EFFECT

Think about how hot a car can get in summer with all the windows closed. The heat gets in but can't get out. A greenhouse works in a similar way. Methane and carbon dioxide are called greenhouse gases because they trap heat in Earth's atmosphere. Scientists believe greenhouse gases are making the earth too warm. This warming causes problems such as changing weather patterns and melting ice around the poles.

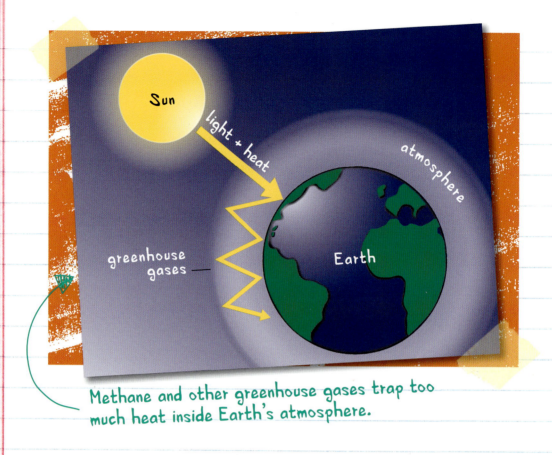

Methane and other greenhouse gases trap too much heat inside Earth's atmosphere.

in climate are normal, but large changes can throw the environment out of whack."

"How do you keep the methane from escaping into the atmosphere?"

"We trap the gas and change it into usable energy. Wastes and manure are pumped from the lagoons into the **biodigester**," he says, pointing to a large sealed tank sticking out of the ground. "Bacteria already present in the waste helps separate the waste into solids and gases. We remove the solids, and the gases—mostly methane and carbon dioxide—are sent through the pipe so we can use them."

I tell Dave the gas pipe looks pretty small, but he says that gases squeeze through easily. Gas molecules are so spread out that there's plenty of room to push them together.

Something clicks in my mind, and I think about the soda in Mrs. Jones's classroom. The bubbles are a gas squeezed into the drink. I turn my thoughts back to Dave. I want to know how he uses this gas.

"We burn the methane from the biodigester to help create the electricity that heats this barn and runs our milking machines. I sell any gas we don't use to the electric company," he says.

"How did you get started?"

"We just started using this collection system. I measured and recorded the methane levels here for five years before I invested in the digester," Dave says. "I had to become a scientist farmer."

"You're a gas scientist," I reply. "You let the properties of gases work for you, and you help the environment too."

I leave thinking of Mrs. Jones's balloon. The air filled up its container—the balloon. Our atmosphere is a giant container filled with all sorts of gases. I'm looking forward to my next stop. I can't wait to find out more about what gases do when they are heated. ★

I've traveled to Albuquerque, New Mexico, to watch the Balloon Festival. I meet Joe and Janet Smith at 4:00 a.m. in the festival park. I can see the outline of their hot air balloon stretched flat across the grass. The basket lies sideways.

I ask them why hot air balloons have to launch so early in the morning. Janet says the wind is calmer and the air is cooler, so the hot air in the balloon rises more easily. I nod, and she tells me the balloon and all its parts weigh more than 400 pounds (180 kg). I wonder how the balloon can weigh that much and still float. I watch the crew attach the balloon to the basket with cables. Someone aims a huge fan at the balloon's opening.

"Is he filling it with cold air?" I ask. "I thought it was a hot air balloon."

"We fill the balloon partway with cool air. Then we heat the air, and it expands to fill the balloon," Janet says. As the balloon inflates, I look up.

"What is that thing?" I ask, pointing at a small balloon hovering high above us.

"It's a pibal," Joe replies. "That's a test balloon filled with helium gas. Helium is lighter than air. We can learn a

lot about wind currents by watching how the pibal moves."
He flips open a notebook and shows me some data. "We
record the wind speeds every time we balloon. After a few
flights, we have a feel for the wind currents in the area."

The hot air balloon is partially filled, and a crew
member lights the propane heater that sits directly under
the balloon's opening. It looks like the one on my parents'
gas grill. I watch, amazed, as the balloon slowly lifts away
from the ground. Joe pushes the basket upright and holds
it as the pilot steps in. The pilot takes over the propane

The air inside the balloon is warmer than the air outside
the balloon. Warm air rises, and so does the balloon!

heater. He directs the flame inside the balloon to continue heating the air.

The heated air makes the balloon tug harder at the basket. Joe lets go of the basket, and the balloon hovers and then lifts into the air. The pilot flips the burner on and off to control how fast the balloon rises.

"I still don't completely understand why the balloon floats," I say.

"We heat the cold air inside the balloon," Joe replies. "Heat makes the air molecules move faster. They collide faster and speed apart, causing the gas to take up more

WHY AIRPLANES FLY

Airplanes must overcome the force of gravity pulling them down. The force opposing gravity is lift. Lift is created by differences in pressures above and below the wings of an airplane. Airplane wings curve, which makes air passing over the top of the wings move faster, while the air under the wings moves more slowly. Faster-moving air creates low pressure, while slower-moving air creates high pressure. Air with a higher pressure pushes harder. This higher air pressure underneath the wings creates the lift that pushes the plane upward. This is Bernoulli's principle, which was discovered by Daniel Bernoulli in the 1700s.

Once off the ground, hot air balloons drift with the wind.

room. But because there are fewer molecules in the same space from all the spreading out, the **density** is less. The air inside the balloon is lighter than the outside, cooler air. The balloon goes up." I ask how the balloon moves sideways.

"The pilot can't control that—only up and down," Janet says. "Wind currents move it sideways. That's why you won't see us ballooning when the wind is over ten miles per hour (16 kmh)."

"How do you make the balloon go down then?" I ask. Joe tells me there's a rip cord that lets hot air out so cooler air can rush in. Cooler air is denser because the molecules are closer together. It's heavier, so the balloon moves down.

"That's why they're called hot air balloons," I say. "Heat expands gases because their molecules move faster and spread out. That means hot air is less dense than cool air. So the balloons rise!"

"Yes, and aren't gases fun?" Janet says. I agree. As I leave, I think about Mrs. Jones and her frozen balloon. The cooled air inside was denser because the molecules weren't so spread out. The balloon shrunk. I wonder if that balloon would expand if I put it in a warm car.

Thinking about hot air rising reminds me of the egg in the bottle. Mrs. Jones dropped a burning match into the bottle, so it must have heated the air inside. The gas expanded, pushing against the egg. When the match went out, the air inside the bottle cooled. The cooler air molecules moved closer together, reducing the air pressure in the bottle. But what pushed the egg into the bottle? ★

Today I'm at an auto testing lab in Fullerton, California. I'm meeting automotive engineer Daniel Lee. On the phone, he told me he works with gases, but I'm not sure how cars use gases. They use gasoline, but that's a liquid. When I arrive, Daniel takes me back to the lab and asks if I like explosions. He says that's what I'll see today because he tests car engines.

"Do car engines use gases?" I ask.

"Absolutely," he says. "Cars run on energy produced by heated gas. In an engine, **pistons** move up and down inside small **cylinders**. The piston starts at the top of the cylinder, then moves down to let in air. It also lets in a tiny drop of

EAT AN EXPLOSION!

A popcorn seed has a hard, strong outer shell to protect the starch, oil, and tiny bit of water inside it. The starch is food for the seed when it begins to grow. Heating a popcorn seed boils the bit of water inside, turning it to vapor. This gas expands until the shell explodes from the gas's pressure, turning the popcorn seed inside out. This quick release of pressure boils the starch and releases it as foam. The foam hardens into the popcorn puff.

gasoline. Then the piston moves up again, compressing the air and gasoline. Gases are easy to compress because their molecules are so spread out. But as the space decreases, the pressure inside the cylinder increases. When the piston reaches the top of the cylinder, a spark ignites the fuel. A little explosion occurs, heating the air. The heated air wants to expand, but the piston is in the way. The increased pressure pushes the piston back down. Then the process repeats. The energy produced by the gas pushing the piston runs the car."

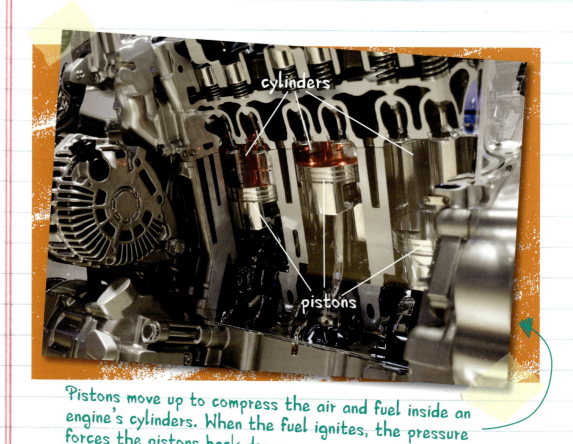

Pistons move up to compress the air and fuel inside an engine's cylinders. When the fuel ignites, the pressure forces the pistons back down.

"Does the compression process ever go wrong?" I ask.

"Yes, it can. An engine's parts work as a group to make a tight seal where the explosion takes place. The seal allows pressure to build. When parts get worn, the seal breaks. Since gases exert an equal pressure on all of their surroundings, the compressed air escapes where the seal is broken, and pressure is lost. You don't get the same power with your gas and fuel mix. It's not as efficient."

Compressed gases exert lots of pressure, but all gases have pressure of their own. I remember the egg slipping into the bottle. The match in the bottle heated the air inside, making it push on the egg, just like the heated air inside a car engine pushes the piston. As the flame went out and the air cooled, the pressure inside the bottle lessened. The greater outside air pressure pushed the egg into the bottle. Who knew that gases pushed things around?

I examine the model engine in Daniel's lab so I can see the cylinders and where the mix is compressed. I move the pistons myself, picturing tiny explosions. It's time to go.

Daniel shows me out. I head home to organize everything, and I plan to visit Mrs. Jones again. I think she knew I'd figure it out as I learned more. I'm amazed at what gases can do and how they affect our world. Writing my article should be a breeze! ★

Way to go! You've learned about gases and how they act. You know gases have no shape or size. They take the shape of their container, even one as big as Earth's atmosphere. You've seen that gases exert pressure, and their molecules constantly move in straight lines until they collide. Heated gases expand, and cooled gases contract. You've seen that gases are easy to compress, and their pressure grows as they are compressed. You've also learned that gases are all around, and they affect the lives of everyone on Earth. Congratulations on your success!

CONSIDER THIS

★ Explain why a hot air balloon filled with cold air won't rise.

★ Why do gases take the shape of their container?

★ Using what you know about the way gases move, why does it take some time to smell a gas from across the room?

★ Why does the pressure of a gas increase as it is compressed?

★ What are some of the ways gases can be harmful? How can we protect ourselves and our planet from the damage gases can cause?

Gases can lift you up and help you travel around the world.

biodigester (bye-oh-dye-JEST-ur) equipment for changing methane gas and other gases into fuel

compress (kuhm-PRES) to squeeze a substance so it fits in a small space

cylinder (SIL-uhn-dur) a tube-shaped part in a car engine

density (DEN-si-tee) how heavy or light a thing is for its size

greenhouse gas (GREEN-hous gas) a gas such as methane or carbon dioxide that traps heat in Earth's atmosphere, causing the atmosphere to warm

methane (METH-ane) a colorless, odorless gas that can be burned and acts as a greenhouse gas

molecule (MAH-luh-kyool) the smallest particle of a material that has the same properties as that material

piston (PIS-tuhn) a shaft that fits inside an engine's cylinder and moves up and down

water vapor (WAW-tur vay-pur) the gas state of water

LEARN MORE

BOOKS

Kjelle, Marylou Morano. *The Properties of Gases*. New York: PowerKids Press, 2007.

Meyer, Susan. *Gases and Their Properties*. New York: Rosen Central, 2011.

Mezzanotte, Jim. *Gases*. Milwaukee, WI: Weekly Reader Early Learning Library, 2007.

Royston, Angela. *Solids, Liquids, and Gases*. Chicago, IL: Heinemann Library, 2008.

WEB SITES

Balloon Race

http://www.pbs.org/wgbh/nova/balloon/science/density

Take a hot air balloon trip around the world.

Energy Kids

http://www.eia.doe.gov/kids/energy.cfm?page=environment_about_ghg-basics

Learn more about greenhouse gases and what they do to the environment.

Science Kids

http://www.sciencekids.co.nz/gamesactivities/gases.html

Do some fun experiments with gases online.

POPCORN CRUSH

Use pliers to crush ten to fifteen popcorn seeds before popping a batch of popcorn. Observe what happens when the uncrushed popcorn pops and what happens to the crushed popcorn seeds. Is there a difference in how they pop? What happens to the crushed and uncrushed seeds? Why did this happen?

BALLOON BLOWUP

Explore the effects of hot and cold air on balloons. Begin by blowing up two identical balloons to an equal size. Check their size by measuring them with a tape measure. Put one balloon in a warm place, such as inside a car on a hot day. Place the other balloon in the refrigerator. Keep them there an equal amount of time. When you remove them, quickly measure their sizes again. What happened to the two balloons?

INDEX

ABOUT THE AUTHOR

Shirley Duke taught at the elementary and secondary levels for many years before becoming a children's writer. She holds a master's degree in education and a bachelor's degree in biology. Her publications include both fiction and nonfiction. She lives with her husband in Garland, Texas.

ABOUT THE CONSULTANTS

Dr. Griff Jones is a clinical associate professor at the University of Florida. He has two decades of experience teaching students of all ages about science. Dr. Jones has received national-level recognition for his efforts as a K-adult science educator, including the Presidential Award for Excellence in Science Teaching in 1998.

Gail Saunders-Smith is a former classroom teacher and Reading Recovery teacher leader. Currently she teaches literacy courses at Youngstown State University in Ohio. Gail is the author of many books for children and three professional books for teachers.